CW01065249

STOCK TRADING

BUY LOW
SELL HIGH

*The Definitive Guide For
Beginner Traders In The
Stock Market*

King Peterson

Copyright © 2020 King Peterson

All Rights Reserved

Copyright 2020 By King Peterson - All rights reserved.

The following book is produced below with the goal of providing information that is as accurate and reliable as possible. Regardless, purchasing this eBook can be seen as consent to the fact that both the publisher and the author of this book are in no way experts on the topics discussed within and that any recommendations or suggestions that are made herein are for entertainment purposes only. Professionals should be consulted as needed prior to undertaking any of the action endorsed herein.

This declaration is deemed fair and valid by both the American Bar Association and the Committee of Publishers Association and is legally binding throughout the United States.

Furthermore, the transmission, duplication or reproduction of any of the following work including specific information will be considered an illegal act irrespective of if it is done electronically or in print. This extends to creating a secondary or tertiary copy of the work or a recorded copy and is only allowed with express written consent from the Publisher. All additional right reserved.

The information in the following pages is broadly considered to be a truthful and accurate account of facts and as such any inattention, use or misuse of the information in question by the reader will render any resulting actions solely under their purview. There are no scenarios in which the publisher or the original author of this work can be in any fashion deemed liable for any hardship or damages that may befall them after undertaking information described herein.

Additionally, the information in the following pages is intended only for informational purposes and should thus be thought of as universal. As befitting its nature, it is presented without assurance regarding its prolonged validity or interim quality. Trademarks that are mentioned are done without written consent and can in no way be considered an endorsement from the trademark holder.

Table of Contents

PART I

Chapter 1: Understanding the Fundamentals of Day Trading

As mentioned in the introduction, day trading is a short-term investment approach. This approach is based mainly on stocks. As such, day traders trade stocks of publicly-traded companies in the United States. While it is possible to trade the stock of international companies, they would have to be listed for public trading in the United States. So, for the purpose of this book, we are going to be focusing on the United States stock market.

Traditionally, the only way an average person could invest in the stock market was through a brokerage firm. This meant that the average investor had to go to their local bank or investment firm to open up a brokerage account. From there, a stockbroker or professional money manager would handle their investment capital.

This is still done today. The difference is that technology has now enabled us to cut out the middleman, that is, we no longer need to take a trip down to a bank or investment firm to open up an investment account. In fact, you can do this now from the comfort of your home. Thanks to the internet, there is no need to seek out the services of professional stockbrokers and money managers.

It should be noted that when you choose to make your own investment decisions, you need to be cognizant of what you are doing. Sure, it may seem like it's just a matter of buying and selling stocks, but there's more to it than that. The fact of the matter is you need to be aware of how the process works.

That's why we're here!

As such, folks who wish to invest their money themselves can become a "day trader." This term refers to those investors who open and close their positions within the same trading day. This means that you can zero stocks when you start your trading day, buy up a bunch of stocks, and then sell everything off before you close shop for the day.

This is the classic definition.

There is an expanded definition that considers leaving open positions overnight. However, we will not encourage you to do so in this book as leaving positions open overnight can be quite dangerous, particularly due to the increase in trading volume that occurs at the beginning of each trading day.

The reason why day trading exists is because trading occurs from Monday to Friday from 9 am to 4 pm. This is when stock exchanges are open. A stock exchange is the physical place in which trading takes place. In the olden days, this was the trading floor that is commonly featured in films. Nowadays, the building still exists, and it still houses offices. However, most of the trading is done by computers. The most famous stock exchange is the New York Stock Exchange located on Wall Street. Yet, it is not the only one. There are others in Chicago, Philadelphia, and Miami.

At this point, it should be noted that we are not endorsing day trading as a full-time job. While you could certainly do it, it is not advisable to quit your day job and become a full-time day trader until you have the experience and the confidence needed to replace your current income source. Nevertheless, when you do build up the skills and experience, you can make a lot more money trading than working at any job (unless it was a very high-paying job).

Characteristics of a Day Trader

There is no need to have special skills or training to become a day trader. Sure, it would help if you had a degree in finance or economics, but there is nothing that would keep you from becoming a successful day trader is you didn't have a degree in these areas.

In fact, the most successful day traders are the folks that are able to understand the fundamentals of the markets and how to manage the trading platform. Beyond that, all you really need is common sense. Unfortunately, this isn't something that is taught in graduate programs. Most professionals with advanced degrees get caught up in complex models that don't always reflect the fundamentals of the markets.

This is where anyone with common sense can really flourish. When you understand how the market works, you won't have to figure out any complex models and systems. Everything you need to know is laid out for you. All you need to do is make sense of it all.

Nevertheless, there are some personal qualities that day traders need to have. Firstly, all good traders need to be patient. Being "trigger happy" is not a good way to make money when trading. Secondly, traders should be cautious. This means that you need to study your strategy before putting it into practice. The more you study, the easier it will be to avoid making big mistakes. Thirdly, successful traders are proactive. This means that they are able to anticipate movements in the market before they happen. This is a quality that is developed over time. But when this instinct is fully sharpened, it can lead to significant profits well before the majority of investors wake up and smell the coffee.

So, do take the time to ponder these characteristics. By embracing them, you will be giving yourself the best chance to be successful.

Day Trading as a Full-Time Career

Earlier, we mentioned that while it is not advisable to quit your day job to pursue day trading full time, it is entirely possible to make a career out of it. In fact, there are plenty of stories out there of folks who have made this transition.

Generally speaking, it is perfectly possible to do so. However, this depends on your ability to learn the ropes effectively and make consistent returns. Since day trading is based on the stock market and its fluctuations, consistent returns aren't always guaranteed. This is why the learning curve in trading can be steep at times. Nevertheless, if you are able to consistently deliver on the results that you need to finance your lifestyle, you could certainly make a career out of it.

Most folks start out trading in their free time. As they gain momentum, they devote more and more time to it. Eventually, they are able to supplement their income quite well. This gives them the flexibility to work less hours at their regular job or are transitioning into a full-time investing career. The important thing to keep in mind here is that making day trading a full-time career eventually becomes a job of its own. Your challenge would be to manage your time so that you can make money while enjoying the flexibility that comes with trading.

The Difference Between Day, Swing, and Position Trading

By definition, day trading is a short-term investment approach. As stated earlier, day trading involves opening and closing positions within the same trading day. On the surface, this seems like you won't have too much time to reap the rewards of your investments. However, please be assured that there is money to be made in such a short time period. As a matter of fact, most of the action happens at the beginning and end of the trading day.

This is why we mentioned that it could be dangerous to leave positions open overnight. You see, at the start of the trading day, investors place their first trades before the stock exchanges open. This allows them to capitalize on the previous day's closing price. Then, when the market opens, a flood of orders goes through the door. This is why you see investors placing their orders within the first two hours following the open of the market. After those first two hours, the trading volume reduces significantly. It is said that you should trade between 11 am and 2 pm as there isn't much action going on during that time. While that is certainly true, if you are looking to make a quick buck, the truth is there is always money to be made at any time.

In contrast, swing trading enables investors to keep positions open for multiple days but never longer than a full week. So, this means that you could open up your positions on Monday morning and close them up on Friday afternoon. With swing trading, you are giving yourself a chance to cash in swings the market that takes longer than a few hours. In fact, some shifts in the market may take longer than two or three days. This is why you need to set up your position ahead of time. This is what we mean by being proactive.

As for position trading, this is a long-term approach. Now, in the world of investing, "long-term" is a rather broad term. In some cases, there are investors who choose to hold on to positions for years. They are keen on holding on to the stock of prime companies as a means of preserving their wealth. Additionally, holding on to stocks for extended time periods enables investors to collect dividends from profits. For the purpose of this book, we are going to be looking at position investing as a long-term approach that spans any period greater than a week. Typically, most position investors hold open positions for periods ranging from a week to roughly 200 days. Later on, we'll discuss the fundamentals of this timeframe in great detail.

Benefits of Day Trading

Day trading can be an excellent way of supplementing your income. At first, you shouldn't expect it to replace your primary source(s) of income. Nevertheless, day trading can provide you with the extra income you need to pay down debt, save up for important purchases, or eventually make a career switch. Beyond this, there are clear benefits to day trading.

Consider these:

- Day trading is flexible. This means that you can trade anytime, anywhere.
- There is no limit to your potential income. When you master the fundamentals, you will find there is no market cap. You can make as much as you possibly can.
- There is no need for large investment capital. You don't need to invest thousands, or even millions, to get started. Just a few hundred dollars is enough to get started.
- It's fully automated. The trading platforms that you will be using are fully automated. This means that everything you need to do is there on your computer.

- You have access to a wide range of stocks and other financial products. You are only limited by your understanding of the products you are looking to trade.

- You don't pay commissions on each trade. There are costs per trade and maintenance fees. However, you cut out the middleman as there is no need to pay stockbrokers.

On the surface, day trading has a number of advantages. By taking full advantage of them, you can watch your capital grow quickly and easily. Best of all, you don't need to make any sacrifices to get started.

Drawbacks of Day Trading

As with anything, there are also drawbacks. This means that there are things you need to look out for. Nevertheless, day trading can be a great way for you to make money if you are wary of the following drawbacks.

- There are fees to be paid. These pertain to maintenance fees for the trading platform you are using in addition to the fees per trade that you need to pay. If you take advantage of bundles and other special offers, you can reduce the costs associated with trading.

- You have to pay taxes. Yes, there are taxes that need to be paid on the profits you make. So, it's best to take a look at what taxes you may be liable for in your state. Generally speaking, you'll be on the hook for capital gains tax. So, do keep an eye out for this.

- Time and study are needed to master the craft. Yes, you will have to invest time and effort in learning the ropes of day trading. Still, it's time well spent. If you have a busy lifestyle, then it's important to take this into account before signing up.

- There is always risk involved in trading. When you engage in day trading or any type of investing, there is always risk involved. This is why studying trading is important as it will help you to manage the potential risk that may come from investing.

Through careful study and attention, you can compensate for these drawbacks. In fact, you can transform them into new opportunities. So, do take the time to evaluate these drawbacks, so you are not caught off-base.

Day Trading Equities

The term "equities" refers to stocks. As such, when you day trade equities, you are focusing specifically on stocks. While this means that you can branch out to other types of financial assets, the main focus of your investment endeavors is stocks. Of course, the world of stocks is quite large. There is any number of companies and industries you can focus on. That why it's important to narrow your focus on a group of stocks or a sector that you feel comfortable dealing with.

In this regard, many day traders narrow their focus on a single industry when first starting out. Since there is a considerable number of companies in the market, trying to capture them all can be quite difficult. So, some investors like to focus on tech companies. Others like to focus on manufacturing, retail, or even gas and oil. When you narrow your focus to a single industry or group of stocks, you facilitate your understanding of the dynamics in that particular sector. This makes it easier for you to gain specific insight into the movements in prices for these specific companies.

Other investors choose to focus on specific stock indices. A stock index is a grouping of stocks by industry, size, or turn of business. The largest stock index in the United States is the Dow Jones Industrial Average. The Dow Jones is a collection of the 30 largest publicly-traded companies in America. Its purpose is to track the performance of these companies and translate their performance into a round number that investors can visualize. This is the number that you see on the nightly news. For example, the Dow reached a high of over 29,000 points in February of 2020. This marked a new record for the Dow.

Other major stock indices include the NASDAQ. This index groups the major tech companies in the United States. Also, the S&P 500 is a collection of the 500 biggest companies traded in America. There are several other indices that you can use as a reference. However, the three mentioned in this chapter are the industry standard and serve a yardstick for investors. If you are keen on tracking one of these indices, you can do so as a means of giving you a specific target to shoot for. Otherwise, you may find yourself trying to cast a wide net. In the world of investing, that's not necessarily a good thing.

Day Trading Options

Options are both a tool and an instrument. The term "options" refers to a very specific type of contract in which investors set a number of parameters that guide a transaction. For instance, a common parameter is time. This means that investors set a specific time limit for a transaction to happen. A common timeframe is 30 days. This means that the transaction, be it buy or sell, will be activated at the 30-day mark.

The purpose of an option is to agree on price and/or quantity in advance of a deal taking place. This allows investors to lock in a certain price or amount, thereby giving them the assurance that they have the assets they need at the specified time or price. It's also important to note that a common parameter for options is price. Thus, a transaction may be triggered by a certain price point. This implies that if a stock hits a certain price, a buy or sell order is automatically enacted.

As a day trader, you can buy and sell these contracts for a price. Likewise, you can take out one of these contracts in order to hedge your position, particularly in uncertain times. The great thing about an options contract is that you don't actually have to go through with it. This is why it's called an "option." If you should choose not to go through with the deal, even when the specific parameters have been reached, all you would lose is the cost for underwriting the contract.

Day Trading FOREX

FOREX is the largest and most liquid market in the world. In this market, you are literally buying and selling currencies. The dynamic in this market is rather different from that of the stock market as you are dealing with the currency of sovereign nations. This means that there are socioeconomic factors that influence the valuation of currency in addition to the fundamental market forces. Still, FOREX is an exciting market that offers investors very short-term gains. Often, FOREX traders open and sell positions within a matter of minutes. However, in those few minutes, they can make a substantial gain.

It should be noted that "volume" is the name of the game in FOREX. The reason for this is due to the fact that you may only make pennies on each trade. But the size of your position is what amplifies the gains. Moreover, if you engage in high-frequency trading, that is, make a large number of transactions in a short timeframe, you can rack up small gains to the point where they are considerably large.

Also, FOREX is a 24-hour market. This means that it never closes. This is why many day traders also choose to engage in FOREX; it gives them the opportunity to continue trading even after the stock exchanges have closed. For those who have full-time jobs or busy schedules, FOREX offers an opportunity to trade at any time they choose. This is why FOREX is truly the weapon of choice for busy investors.

Chapter 2: Essentials of Day Trading

Once you have made up your mind to begin day trading, the next step is to begin doing research on how you can get started. Getting started is relatively easy. Gaining access to the market doesn't require a great deal of work. In fact, it's a rather easy process. The hard part is learning the ropes of the trading system that you will be using.

In this chapter, we are going to be focusing on the essentials of day trading. This means that we are going to be discussing what you need to do to get ready for your very first trade. Please bear in mind that day trading requires some careful study and learning early on. But once you get the hand of the trading system, it will be rather easy for you to navigate the waters of the trading world.

The hardest part of day trading is the research that does into determining the right stocks to pick and which are the best options for you to make money. This is important to note as not all stocks are created equal. The so-called "blue chip" stocks belong to companies that have a great track record. These are companies that have a long-lasting reputation and proven performance. As such, they are expensive and highly sought-after. Consequently, it's important for you to be careful with penny stocks. These are companies whose share price is less than five dollars. These stocks generally belong to companies that have serious financial or administrative issues but are yet to be liquidated. In essence, they are hanging on for dear life.

When you commit to regular research and study surrounding stocks, you will find that it's quite straightforward to pick winners from losers. The challenge then becomes entering and exiting trades at the right time. Learning to time your movements within trades is usually a matter of practice and experience. As you become familiar with the technical analysis tools that you can use to interpret price action, you'll be able to ascertain when to entre and when to leave. As a result, you can quickly "time" your moves so that you can make money every time.

To get started as a day trader, you need to open a brokerage account. This account will enable you to enter the trading floor (albeit virtually) so that you can begin buying and selling stocks.

Opening a New Brokerage Account

It's important to note that you need to open a brokerage account to trade stocks. This is an essential requirement as an average individual is not licensed to trade stocks. That's what stockbrokers are licensed to do. In addition, you can't simply turn on your computer to buy and sell stocks. To do this, you need to comply with government regulations. These regulations state that only duly licensed financial institutions can actively engage in trading stocks. Therefore, you need to trade through one of these institutions. Otherwise, you won't be able to gain access.

When you open a new account, what you are getting is access to the trading platform. This is the digital space in which traders can interact with one another. This is where all of the action takes place. As a result, you are granted access to this digital space by the financial institution that's running the trading platform.

There are no formal requirements for you to gain access to a day trading platform. The fact is that all you need is to meet the technical requirements of the trading platform and, most importantly, meet the financial requirements of the account you wish to open. Generally speaking, trading accounts can range from as little as $500 to several thousand depending on the level you wish to trade. As a novice investor, it's best to stay away from an account, requiring a large investment capital upon startup. It's better to open up an account that has a low investment capital requirement. The reason for this is simple. When you sink too much money into day trading when you are inexperienced, you may either be too cautious or too brazen. So, it's best to start off small and work your way up. If you are already experienced and have a larger sum on money, you can definitely try your hand at a larger investment capital position early on.

When you go about picking the institution you are going to do business with. Please keep in mind that you'll find one of two types of institutions. First, you have a full-service financial broker and second, a discount broker. The difference between them can be quite significant.

A full-service broker provides users with a full range of services. These services include the use of the trading platform in addition to a host of services such as real-time data, analytics, and other expert advice. In some cases, free training sessions are offered as part of the package. But the most important thing you should look for is the free demo account. When you sign up for a full account, you generally get a free trial account in which you can have access to the entire platform without using your capital. This means that you can trade with monopoly money for a few days.

This is something you need to take advantage of. By using the demo account, you'll be able to make mistakes without being concerned about blowing your investment capital. It's a great way to learn the ropes and be ready for the real thing.

As far as costs are concerned, full-service accounts generally come with an annual membership fee. While this fee may be waived when you sign up, you'll eventually have to pay some kind of maintenance fee. That's what keeps the lights on for these platforms. Additionally, you'll have to pay a fee per trade. When you deal with these types of brokers, the fees per trade are usually low. They will range anywhere from a few cents per trade to about a couple of dollars. It's important for you to be aware of how much you would be paying per trade. That way, you can manage your costs and calculate your real profits.

Then there are discount brokers. Discount brokers sell you access to the bare-bones platform. So, you can use the fully functional platform but without the bells and whistles. This usually means no access to analytics or real-time data. You'll have access to charts and graphs, but they are generally on a delay. So, you'll have to find another information service that can give you access to real-time data. It should also be noted that discount brokers have very low membership fees (in some cases they don't), but you'll need to keep a certain minimum balance in your account (which can be a bit high at times) while also a higher fee per trade. Be on the lookout for these fees per trade as they can be quite high at times. However, most discount brokers sell trade bundles. For instance, you'll get 10 trade for $2.99. Take advantage of these bundles as they'll help you keep your costs in check.

Another important thing about discount brokers is that they don't always allow you to have the demo account. So, if you are keen on starting out with a discount broker, please note that you will go live right from the start. As such, you need to be ready to trade for real.

Placing Your First Trades

Once you have gone about choosing your broker and trading system platform, you are ready to make your first trades. Making trades is a pretty straightforward process. You buy low and sell high. That's the logic behind it. However, the process itself can be a bit tricky. So, it's important to learn the basics of placing your first trades

In this section, we are going to look at how you can make your first trades happen. Please bear in mind that doing the tutorial until you are completely familiar with the dynamics of the trading system platform is essential. Otherwise, you won't be able to get the most out of the tools available to you.

Bid price

The first thing to note when placing a trade is the price action that occurs among investors and traders. Everyone has their own agenda, so to speak. What this means is that buyers want to get the lowest price will sellers want to get the highest price they can. Eventually, both parties meet somewhere in the middle. When this occurs, a transaction happens. And yes, there are times when they can't meet in the middle. In those cases, transactions stall until someone budges or orders are withdrawn.

With that in mind, the bid price is the price that buyers put up for a specific stock they want to purchase. The term "bid" is used as this is not the final price they are willing to pay. This is merely an offer that buyers make. In a manner of speaking, it's like an auction. If the seller is willing to take that price, then a match is made.

Most buyers are comfortable with the idea of going a bit higher if they believe they will find value at a higher price point. Then again, there are instances in which buyers panic and are willing to pay anything for an asset. If you are the holder in this situation, you can set your price and get paid accordingly. Also, bid prices are a reflection of what investors believe an asset is worth. So, don't be surprised if you see buyers paying far lower amounts than you might expect based on market averages.

Ask price

As for ask prices, well, the term speaks for itself; it's an asking price. In the ask price, sellers establish a price they would like to get for the stock they hold. If there is a match, then the sale occurs. If the price is not matched by any other investors, then the order goes unfulfilled. Therefore, the ask price is a parameter just like the bid price is. In the end, the convergence of both prices is what makes the market function.

It should be noted that in a healthy market, there is very little divergence among prices. This means that the price action is relatively stable. Naturally, there are fluctuations in the market. But on the whole, there is very little change. So, investors have a predictable range in which prices move. This is called a "range." As such, trading within a range can offer you the opportunity to make predictable gains. All you have to do is recognize the signals.

Best Time to Trade

In the world of day trading, the bulk of the action is generally clumped into two separate moments. These are the moments in which trading volume picks up. By "trading volume," we are referring to the number of transactions that take place during a specific timeframe. As such, there are specific times of day in which trading volume increases while there are other times when the action settles down. When you recognize these times, you can make a certain profit from them.

The best times to trade are right at the opening and closing of the trading. The reason for this is the increased trading volume. Think about it this way: if you go fishing, your chance of catching fish would be when the stream is busiest and not when it's quietest. This is the same logic that applies here.

Before the start of the trading day, most investors set up their positions so that they are quickly carried out when trading officially opens. This is where the flood of orders comes in. The flood of orders is based on the previous day's close. For instance, is the stock of company ASD closed lower than usual, there might be a flood of purchase orders at the beginning of the next trading day. This is a point where you could get in on the action. By the same token, if the price of ASD closed higher than normal, there might be a flurry of sell order at the outset of the day. As such, it would be a bad time to get in. Rather, it would be best to get in after the action has died down.

At the end of the trading day, most investors look to liquidate their positions. So, it's a perfect time to sell. If you are holding any open positions, you can set up your trades so that they go through during the final hour or so, leading up to the close of the markets. That way, you can make some profits at the tail end of the day while ensuring that you close all positions before wrapping up for the day.

This is the dynamic of day trading in a nutshell. Throughout the day, you can open positions if the price is right while also enabling you to make profits should conditions be favorable. A good rule of thumb to keep in mind is that there is no reason why you should enter a trade unless you are sure about what you are doing. If you are unsure about anything, it's always best to stay away. You would be better off sitting out a trade rather than taking a plunge and getting hammered.

Risk Management

Risk is an inherent part of trading. There is no question that any type of investing comes with its dose of risk. This implies that you need to be mindful of the role risk plays in your investment activity. On the whole, risk is about understanding what could go wrong and what you can do to remedy it. Therefore, your understanding of these conditions will help you to avoid catastrophic mistakes.

So, let's take a look at five helpful rules when considering risk in your day trading endeavors:

1. **Don't put all your eggs in one basket**. When you put too many of your resources into a single trade, you are opening up the door to trouble. So, it's best to limit your exposure to risk by setting a maximum amount of funds invested in a single trade.

2. **Invest in companies you are familiar with**. If you plan on investing in a company you have never heard of, you might be asking for trouble. So, always make sure that you do a cursory check on any company you're thinking about trading.

3. **Avoid following the herd**. When you hear folks talking about the hottest stock at the moment, you're already too late. The best time to trade stocks is when no one is talking about them. You can figure out what these stocks are by doing your research.

4. **Be careful with the "fear of missing out**. Often, you hear investors talking about the next big thing. So, it's natural to assume that if you don't get in, you're going to miss out on a great

opportunity. However, there comes a time when you get into an asset just because you're afraid if you don't, others will think you're crazy. This is why you need to make your own decisions, even if that means going against the herd.

5. **Make sure you check out the broker you are doing business with**. Always ensure that when you sign up for a new investment account, you double-check on the broker you have chosen. If you find that there's something shady or not quite right about them, don't sign up. It's better to be skeptical rather than getting burned.

Golden Rules of Money Management

In order to hedge risk, you need to follow the golden rules of money management. So, here are three rules which have proven to stand the test of time. By following them, you can ensure that your portfolio will be safe and sound.

1. **Limit your positions to 1% or 2% of your total investment capital**. This rule calls for moderation. So, never place more than 2% of your total portfolio on a single trade. While you can invest the entire sum of your capital, make sure it stays under the 2% threshold on individual trades.

2. **Cut your losses**. When a deal goes south, always make sure to exit before you dig yourself deeper into the hole. Whenever you try to hold on just a little bit longer in hopes of having the price bounce back, you may end up losing more money in the process. So, as

soon as you see prices heading south, cut your losses. You'll be able to make up those losses later on.

3. **Keep cool**. It's very easy to let your emotions get the best of you. For instance, you might find that you are quick to anger when you lose money on a deal. By the same token, you might think you are invincible when you go on a hot streak. By keeping a level head, you'll be able to make objective decisions every time you enter a deal.

With these golden rules, you'll never go wrong. So, do your best to keep a level head. You'll find that it's easier to manage situations every time the action gets hot and heavy.

Basic Technical Analysis Tools for Day Traders

Technical analysis is the study of the behavior of stocks through the use of quantitative analysis tools. These tools allow you to obtain objective information that you can use to make sound investment decisions. Without them, you would be basing your decisions on nothing more than hunches. So, it's best to do your best to utilize these tools. Here are three of the most important tools you will use to help you make sound decisions.

1. **Moving average**. The moving average is the average price of a stock over a given period of time. Most charts present the moving

average on a daily basis. This means that the price listed reflects the average price of the course of a trading day. The most common measures are the 20, 50, and 200-day moving average. By studying these measures, you'll be able to analyze the overall behavior of the stock's prices.

2. **Trend**. The trend is the direction in which price is heading. Trend can be bullish (increasing) or bearing (falling). When you are able to identify trends, you'll be able to see where the price of the stock is heading. This can be an indication that it's time to buy or it's time to sell. Charting software will calculate this automatically for you. So, make sure you see this line whenever you look at charts.

3. **Significant levels**. These levels refer to the "ceiling" and the "floor" of a stock's price. The ceiling, or resistance level, is a psychological barrier that is reflected in the maximum price that investors are willing to pay. When you look at a chart, you'll notice a resistance level when the price of the stock seems to reach a certain mark and then fall back down. By the same token, a floor, or support level, the lowest level a stock's price will fall. This means that investors feel that this is the lowest price for that stock. Therefore, they buy when the price reaches this point. In other words, this is the lowest point a stock's price will reach during the timeframe you are analyzing.

These three tools are essential in evaluating a stock you are looking to buy. The moving average will help you determine both trend and significant levels. With this, you will be able to determine the entry and exit points of your trades. At the end of the day, you'll be able to make informed decisions regarding the deals you plan to make.

Using the moving average to enter and exit a trade

A simple way in which you could use the moving average to enter and exit a trade is called the "crossover" strategy. In this strategy, you need to pay attention to the price of the stock itself and the moving average. When the actual price of the stock crosses over the moving average, you have a signal of a potential trend reversal. Depending on the nature of the reversal, it would either be time to get in out get out.

- In a bearish trend, if the price becomes higher than the moving average, then you have signal in which the bearish trend may suddenly turn into a bullish one. This would be the time to buy. That way, you can capitalize on the gains that rising, bullish trend would make. The ideal time to buy would be right at the point of crossover. To do this, you need to track the moving average and the current price of the stock. When this cross over occurs, you can place your trade and catch the upswing.

- In a bullish trend, if the price dips below the moving average, then you have a signal of a potential downturn. In this case, you need to pay close attention to the actual point in which the price falls under the moving average. When this occurs, you are at the right time to sell. This is the highest point in the trend. Therefore, if you wait any longer, you will miss out on potential gains.

It should be noted that the most common measure taken here is the 20-day moving average. However, you could compare the 10-day, 20-day and 50-day moving averages to get confirmation of trend reversal.

Chapter 3: Choosing the Best Stocks for Your Portfolio

Knowing how to choose the right stocks is an art form. Many gurus have made their livelihood claiming they know the right stocks to purchase at any given time. In fact, they are keen on pointing out when you should buy and when you should sell. They don't all have perfect track records, but some get it right more often than not.

The issue with picking stocks is that you don't really know if these gurus have an agenda. After all, who knows if they are being paid to promote their own stocks? This is true quite often. You find these gurus promoting companies that they have some kind of stake in. So, you should always take stock advice with a grain of salt.

In this chapter, we are going to focus on the tools you can use to make your own stock picks. Best of all, you don't need to depend on so-called "expert" advice. In fact, all you need is reliable data. Then, with the right analytical tools, you can go ahead and make fairly accurate assumptions based on the information you see. That makes stock picking a fairly straightforward process.

Company Financials

All good investors need to have a solid understanding of company financials. Now, it helps if you have an accounting degree. But you don't need one in order to understand the major points of a company's financials. On the whole, there are two financial statements you need to become familiar with: a balance sheet and a profit and loss statement. Other financial statements are important, but they aren't nearly as important as these two.

The reason why the balance sheet is so important is that it provides a general overview of a company's financial situation. In that statement, you can find the overall health and growth potential. Any possible issues will be reflected in this statement, for instance, high levels of debt. As for the profit and loss (P&L) statement, you will find that it shows how much money the company is making and how much it's actually profiting. This is important to note as there are companies with enormous revenues but very poor profits.

From these two statements, you can use the following financial indicators to determine the health and growth potential of a company. If you are keen on doing your research, you may find some hidden gems that might have been overlooked by other investors.

Company revenue

This indicator is quite useful in determining a company's health. However, it's not an exact measure as not all companies have similar earnings. Naturally, some companies earn a lot more than others. In this regard, a good comparison would be within the industry that the company operates in. For instance, you are evaluating a mining stock. So, it's important to compare the company you are studying with others in the same sector.

Additionally, revenue needs to grow in order for a company to show potential. If you find that revenue is stagnant, then there has to be a reason for this. If you cannot find a logical reason for it, then chances are the company is being mismanaged. In this case, it's best to stay away. A good, healthy growth rate is anything above 10% annually. Although, be careful if a company shows astronomical growth rates. Yes, they look great in the short run but are most likely unsustainable in the long term. This is why looking at companies with a solid track record always makes the most sense. If you are looking at a relatively new company, then be wary.

Earnings Per Share

This indicator provides a much clearer picture of where a company is headed. Simply put, earnings per share refers to the profit divided by the number of shares outstanding. Now, this indicator is not the same as dividends. Dividends are a percentage of after-tax profits that are distributed to shareholders. Earnings per share are just a gross measure of the profits divided by the number of shares. This helps provide a better indication of what shareholders can expect in terms of the company's performance.

When looking at this indicator, you can get a much more even comparison across all companies as profits are universal regardless of the cash amounts. So, if a company is making a 20% profit, this is a measure that can be compared with other companies across the board.

Return on Equity

"Equity" is the accounting term for capital; in other words, the number of resources a company has invested in its production processes. This indicator is simple yet effective in determining the overall performance of a company. All you need to do is that the after-tax profit and divide it by the company's equity. So, if the company profited $100 and has a total equity of $100, then the company is obtaining a return of $1 for every $1 of equity. This would be a phenomenal return. Generally speaking, the dollar amount for this indicator is pennies on the dollars' worth of equity. Nevertheless, it allows investors and analysts to judge the efficiency with which equity is being utilized in the company.

Analyst Recommendations

Analysts and financial experts are always weighing in on company performance. In particular, there is the "earnings season," in which companies published the audited financial statements. This season occurs several times a year. Each season coincides with the end of every quarter. For instance, Q4 earnings are reported in early February of the following year. Q1 earnings are reported in late April, while Q2 earnings are posted in July. Q3 is reported in October. During this time, analysts pour over the data for major companies looking for cracks. By the same token, analysts also look for positive signals. From here, recommendations are issued. You may find recommendations such as "buy," "sell," or "hold." However, always double-check on what you hear. Don't take experts at face value as you never know if they are off base in their assessments.

Positive earnings

Whenever companies post positive earnings, analysts tend to give them a favorable review. However, if the overall trend indicates that earnings are on the way down, then analysts may issue a warning. This often occurs with large corporations that are subject to changes in the market. As such, analysts may tell investors to proceed with caution.

In the event that a company posts negative earnings for a quarter, analysts may sound the alarm bells. After all, if there is no indication that the company may recover, analysts may recommend investors to abandon ship. So, always be on the lookout for reports during earnings seasons. You may end up running into some truly unexpected surprises.

Earnings forecast

This is a key element that influences the opinions of investors. Earnings forecasts can be issued in one of two ways. First, there is "forward guidance" that is issued by company directors. Forward guidance is what companies tell their investors to expect. In some cases, forward guidance may be bullish; that is, the company's directors expect positive results moving forward. In other cases, forward guidance may indicate caution as company directors may be expecting difficulties ahead.

The other source of forecasts comes from analysts who crunch the numbers. They may see things that the company itself may be unwilling to admit. As a result, analysts would go about issuing their own guidance for investors.

When investors compare both types of forecasts, they can make up their minds about the direction that a company is headed. Now, it should be noted that opinions do not generally diverge; that is, the company is bullish while analysts are bearish. Where opinions generally diverge is in the nature of the direction the company is headed. For example, is analysts believe a company is in trouble, they may be rather serious about it while the company may seem to downplay the situation.

Whenever you are researching a stock, always look for any forward guidance and analysts' forecasts. These elements can help you paint a picture of where that company may be headed in the long run. This could offer you enough forewarning.

Earnings growth

As mentioned earlier, earnings present the best indicator of where a company is headed. When evaluating the potential of a company, always look at the historical growth of a company, and then compare it to projected growth. This comparison should provide you with a clear indication of what to expect. For instance, if a company has demonstrated consistent growth at 5%, a sudden forecast of 20% wouldn't make sense unless there was a valid reason. If this reason is due to something like a new product launch, then you may buy into the hype. However, always be wary of any promises. Companies that have a proven track record of successful product launches can cash in on the expectation of a new product. But those that don't have a good track record may leave investors uncertain about its future earnings.

Other Financial Indicators

Here are other indicators that you can use to evaluate the potential for investing in a company. They will always come in handy, particularly when you are unfamiliar with the company itself. Please bear in mind that all of this information is usually available to the public. So, you won't have to crunch the numbers yourself.

1. **PEG Ratio**. The Price/Earnings to Growth Ratio is used to measure the trade-off that exists among the price, the earnings per share, and the expected growth of the company. In general, the PEG should be much higher than the company's actual growth. The rule of thumb here is that a PEG Ration over 1 indicates a company is overvalued while a PEG less than 1 indicates the company is undervalued. This is a good indication of the way investors feel about a particular stock as the price reflects this sentiment.

2. **Industry price earnings**. It is also important to take a look at the earnings across the industry. This is a fair comparison as you can use the industry leaders as a good yardstick for what you can expect from individual companies. If you find that companies are on par, then you have a balanced industry. If you find that a small group of companies dominate the market, then smaller players may not have a lot of room for growth unless they are disruptive, meaning that they can be game-changers.

3. **Dividend**. A dividend is what a company pays out to its shareholders at the end of a fiscal year. This is a percentage that is based on the total after-tax profit of the company. When a company is in trouble, it may choose to suspend its dividend payment either by withholding it, that is paying it out at a later date, or simply not paying it. While the latter is a rather unpopular decision, it can be done to help the company save money while it stabilizes. It should be noted that when a company files for bankruptcy protection, all dividends are suspended.

Please keep in mind that a company's financials are like a blood test for a sick patient. The bloodwork done a patient will reveal what problems the patient might be facing. As such, financial statements provide a similar measure for companies. If the company is in trouble, its financials will reveal this. Of course, there is always the possibility that companies may get creative with their accounting. This is why you need to do your homework on what companies are doing.

On the whole, you can save yourself a great deal of problems by double-checking the facts. It could be that you believed a company was healthy when, in reality, they had issues brewing beneath the surface. Please bear in mind that successful traders and investors are always on the lookout for any information that may tip them off as to what they can expect. So, it's always a good idea to keep your eyes and ears open.

PART II

Part 1: Penny Stocks

Chapter 1: What are Penny Stocks?

Penny stocks are relatively simple, but there are a few tricks that you need to learn in order to make them work for your needs. They represent stocks that are going to have a low price, usually a price that is under a dollar, as well as a smaller market cap that is under $500 million. For the most part, when an investor is working with penny stocks, they are going to be traded off of the traditional exchanges, so you will not find them on the New York Stock Exchange or on the NASDAQ.

So why would you want to choose to work with penny stocks rather than another investment type? There are several reasons to use penny stocks, but they are often used in order to help a company procure the right capital so that the company can grow and become more powerful. Through this market, the company is able to build up the money that is needed so they can grow their business and when you pick the right company, they can make a strong investment for a low cost.

Penny stocks are going to be traded in order to benefit some of the smaller public companies. But if this company does well, and you purchased the stock over the counter before it entered the regular stock exchanges, you could get a great return on investment. Even if the company never makes it over to the regular stock exchange, many of these can still increase their profits and you can earn back on your investment.

Almost all of the penny stocks are going to be sold on over the counter exchanges. This is going to work because many of the larger exchanges are going to have stringent policies before a company can join them and trade. Most of the companies that are in penny stocks will come nowhere near reaching these stringent requirements, plus it costs a lot of money to trade on these exchanges, so it isn't possible for some smaller companies to make it work. Instead of trying to meet some of these requirements or come up with large amounts of money that they don't have, the companies are going to work with the penny stocks to get the funding they need. As the investor, you are able to capitalize on this and get some great stocks, often from some growing companies, for a low price.

As the investor, you need to remember that there will be some risk that comes with going with penny stocks. If you take the time to educate yourself and learn how to avoid some of the major mistakes that come with this investment, you are more likely to make a good income in the process, but keep in mind there are some risks and they are sometimes seen as speculative in nature, rather than as an investment.

Benefits of going with penny stocks

First, let's take some time to look at the benefits of going with penny stocks. Penny stocks could be your next big break. They are a lot of fun to work with because there are a lot of companies who are out there and are looking to use penny stocks as a way to raise capital to grow and become big. If you pick out the right company, you could be one of the first people in on it, and that stock that you got for under a dollar will end up being worth a lot of money down the road if the company does grow.

That is one of the main benefits that come with investing is that there is the potential of making a huge return on investment. You need to make sure that you purchase a stock that is at a low price, which is easy to do in penny stocks, and make sure that it has a good business plan and will survive the market, just like you would with any other investment, and you will see results. Not all companies that are in penny stocks will make it to the big leagues, but many of them can still grow and you can make money from this process.

Many investors like to go with penny stocks because they are exciting and a lot of fun to work with. It is fun and can feel great, to start out with a little bit of money and then move up and see it grow. You may not make a ton of money at first, but penny stocks can help you to start with a small investment and get it to grow. If you want to start out your portfolio and you don't have a ton of money for it, penny stocks can be a great place to start.

The negatives of penny stocks

One of the first negatives that you should be aware of when you are working in penny stocks is that many of the companies on the market are not that good. There are some companies who are really good and just need to make a few tweaks or make a bit more profit before they are able to join the regular stock markets. But many of the companies that you will find in penny stocks didn't get onto the major stock exchanges because they were just bad. You need to learn how to tell the difference between the two if you would like to make an income here.

In addition, the penny stock market is not as reliable as the major stock markets. They are unreliable and they often don't have regulations in place to determine which companies or transactions that go on with them. This doesn't mean that all of the companies are bad on the penny stock market, but since there aren't really a lot of regulations that are in place, many bad companies can sneak through, make up numbers, or hide information and it is really risky picking out the company you want to work with. You will need to be diligent and really do your research to make sure that you are picking out good companies that will earn you money over time.

Penny stocks are really interesting investments to make. They usually have stocks that come in under a dollar each, so they are a good choice for those who have limited money to invest with in the beginning. While you do need to be on guard against some of the bad companies that are able to get onto the penny stock exchange, there are still many great ones that are available that you can pick from and that will help you to make a good return on your investment!

Chapter 2: Picking the Right Trading Strategies

When it comes to working in penny stocks, or any other investment for that matter, one of the most important things that you will need to do is figure out the strategy that you want to use. The strategy is so important because it is going to determine which stocks you will purchase when you will purchase them and sell them, and what research you will do to get the results. There are many great strategies that are available and none of them are necessarily any better or worse than the others, but you will find that picking a strategy and sticking with it, rather than bouncing back and forth between a few, can make all the difference. Some of the best trading strategies that you can use when you want to trade in penny stocks include:

Scalping

This is often a popular strategy to go with because it is pretty simple to use and many beginners like this simplicity. With the idea of scalp trading, you are going to take advantage of some of the inefficiencies that are going on in the market with respect to the spread. The gap between the bid price and the asking price, which is known as the spread, can end up widening or narrowing rapidly throughout time, and even through the day and they are going to create some great selling and buying opportunities that will result in some quick profits.

To scalp, you will need to be good at watching the market and understanding the perfect time to purchase and sale. You can even look at a few markets and see if you are able to find the stocks of a company a little lower than the price of them on the other. You would then purchase the stock at the lower price before moving it over to the other market and selling it for the higher price that is demanded there. You can end up selling the stocks pretty quickly this way and while the profit may only be a little bit on each one, if you purchase quite a few stocks and do this many times, you can make a good profit.

Range trading

When things are going along as normal and all of the other things in the market are even, stocks are often going to trade inside of a set trading range each day. When you use range trading to help you to purchase and sell your penny stocks, you will try to purchase the stock when it is at the bottom of the range, and then when it gets to the top, you will want to sell it. To do this type of trading, you will want to make sure that the stocks have a consistent trading range each day so that you can make some good estimates.

So with this one, you are going to take a look at some of the history of the company, if it is available, and find out what places seem to be the high points of the stock and which ones seem to be the low points. There can be some variations of this each day, but mostly you will notice that the trend stays about the same. You will then take this information to help you make the right purchases on all of your stocks. You will be able to make a purchase of the stock when the market is at the low end of the range and then you can sell the stock when it goes back up before it goes down and you lose out again. This one will require you to spend some time looking through many graphs and charts to get the information, but it can be pretty straightforward and can make you a good profit.

Momentum trading

This is the trading option that you will go with if you are looking to go with some of the trends that are in the market to make a good profit. In basic terms, you are going to use momentum trading or trend trading to purchase a stock when it is trending up, but then you will sell the stock as soon as the trend starts to go back down. This one can be a little less risky compared to some of the others, but you have to constantly be watching the trends and the market to make sure that you get out before all of your investment is gone.

Real-time new trading.

Another option that you are able to go with when you are working on penny stocks is known as real time news trading. This is the one where you are going to have to spend some time reading or watching the news and looking for some clues as to how a market or a particular company is going to do. When you find that some good news is released, you will make the purchase, and then after that little punch up, you will sell the stock. It can also work to protect your investment because if you notice that some bad news is about to happen, you can sell the stocks without losing all the money, and then purchase them again when things settle down.

If you want to use this kind of trading strategy, you will want to make sure that you download a real-time news feed so that you are always getting information in. You also need to be able to understand what each piece of news can mean to the penny stocks that you are working with. You don't want to misunderstand what is going on and end up with selling a stock that was going up or losing out on a stock because you held onto it for too long.

When it comes to picking out the strategy that you want to use for your penny stocks, you will find that there is really no wrong answer. Each person is going to pick out a different strategy to help them out, and what works for one person is not going to work for you. Make sure to check out some of these strategies and then pick the one that works the best for you!

Chapter 3: Getting Started with Your First Trade

When you are ready to get started with your first trade in penny stocks, you will need to take a couple of steps. First, it is important to figure out the broker that you would like to work with. there are many different brokers available out there and many of them have great reputations that can help you to get done with your trading. You should compare a few of them right from the beginning, looking at the features that they offer, as well as some of the fees and costs that they will hand down to you. These will all affect how easy it is to do trades with your broker and how much you will actually make.

Once you have chosen the broker you want to work with, it is time to pick the strategy that you want to work with as well. There are many different strategies, and we discussed a few of them in the chapter above. These can all be successful based on what you would like to get out of the trading. The most important option here is to learn about the different trading strategies for penny stocks and then stick with it.

Many of the investors who end up failing are the ones who just can't seem to stick with the trading strategy that they originally picked. These are the people who will bounce back and forth between a few different options, but they never get familiar or comfortable with just one of them. You can pick any of the strategies that you would like, but you need to make sure that you are sticking with it if you want to see results.

Next on the list is to choose the stocks that you would like to invest in.

This is the part that is going to take some time and you will probably need to use your chosen strategy to help you make the right decisions. When you are picking a stock to invest in, especially when it comes to the penny stock market, you want to make sure that you are being really careful. This is a fantastic market to get into, but if you are not paying attention and doing your research, you will find that your money will be all gone. Many good companies get onto the penny stock market, but so do many bad ones so you have to be diligent if you want to see success.

There are a number of things that you can do to make sure you pick out the right stocks when working in the penny stock market. First, make sure to check out the numbers on your own. Most companies want to gain your trust and will put up their sales information and other relevant things to help you make a good decision to go with them. But since this is not always required of stocks on the penny stock market, there are some that may not provide this information at all and some that will hide factors or fudge the numbers a bit. Doing your own research, and being critical to see if that research is correct, can be a great way to ensure that you are picking out good stocks that will help you earn money.

Always be critical when it comes to picking out a stock on this market. There are too many new investors who are excited to get into the trading business and who want to be able to pick out a company that will make it big. But if you jump in too quickly and don't pay attention to what you are doing while trading, you are going to end up in trouble, and probably losing a lot of money. Make smart decisions, pick out stocks that you think will do well, and always go through and do your own research, and you are sure to see the results.

And finally, after you have chosen your strategy and the stocks that you want to invest in, you have to decide how much you want to invest. Since the penny stock market is often inexpensive, with many of the options coming in at under a dollar, it is pretty affordable for you to make some purchase and get started. But even so, you will want to set the maximum that you want to spend on the stocks, as well as how much you are willing to lose before you get out of the market. Having this plan in place ahead of time can help you to make informed decisions, rather than ones attached to your emotions, and you will see much less risk in the process.

Along the way, if you happen to have any questions about how things are working or what you should do, turning to your broker can be a great idea. They have a lot of experience working in the various investments so they should be able to answer any of the questions or the concerns that come up and they can lead you in the right direction to making a good return on your investment.

PART III

CHAPTER 1: UNDERSTANDING OPTIONS TRADING

Options trading, also known as *binary options trading*, is just like forex and stock trading. However, you do not need to buy currencies or stocks. Instead, you simply predict whether the value of an underlying asset will increase or decrease at a specified time. It is this simplicity of options trading that attract so many investors. It is an option contract that has a fixed payout.

Options trading vs. forex and stock trading

In forex and stocking trading, you buy currencies or stocks and sell them for profit. In options trading, you do not need to buy any trading asset. You only predict whether the price of an underlying asset will be higher or lower than its current price at the expiration date. Also, in forex and stock trading, your profit will depend on the increase in the value of a particular currency or stock that you have purchased. In options trading, the potential profit is fixed and is revealed to you even before you commence a trade.

It is not uncommon for forex and stock traders to wait for weeks and months just to see a little profit from their investment. Many times, they even lose their investment without any chance of getting any profit. This happens when the price of their stocks or currency drops. With options trading, there is always a potential to earn a big amount of profit even when the price of an underlying asset decreases. You do not have to wait for weeks or months; you can double, or even triple, your investment in a few minutes.

Options trading vs. gambling

There are similarities between options trading and gambling. In some jurisdictions, options trading is literally considered gambling. Just like the casino game called *baccarat* where you decide whether the winning hand is *banker* or *player*, in options trading, you will decide whether the value of an underlying asset will rise (Call) or fall (Put) at the expiration time. Just like the table games in the casino, there is a fixed payout for a favorable outcome.

You might be wondering, "Is options trading gambling?" It depends. If you do options trading by relying on guesswork and pure luck, then you are gambling. However, if you consider every wager that you make an investment decision and take the serious effort to study the market and research the different underlying assets being traded, then you are an investor or trader.

It does not really matter whether you see yourself as a gambler or a trader. In the end, what matters is how much profit you have made, if any.

The Basics

Let us move on to the specific parts of options trading. Do not worry; options trading is very easy. You can learn the basics in less than five minutes. It is only like speculating the outcome of a coin flip.

Call vs. Put

There are only two main options to choose from. In options trading, you just have to know whether the outcome will be a *Call* or a *Put*. Simple, right?

Choose the Call option if you predict that the price of an underlying asset will be *above* its current price at the expiration date.

Choose the Put option if you predict that the price of an underlying asset will be *below* its current price at the expiration date.

These two terms are referred to by many names, depending on the trading platform that you use. They are also known as Up/Down, Above/Below, Rise/Fall, and others.

Strike price

This refers to the price at which an asset can be bought or sold at a certain time. In options trading, this simply refers to the Call or Put option. The

Call option is the value at which the underlying asset can be bought, while the Put option is when it can be sold at a specified time.

Expiration time

The expiration time, or simply expiry time, signifies the end of a trading period. This is also the time when you can determine whether or not you have made the right investment decision. Therefore, this is the moment when you will experience a profit or a loss.

In-the-money vs. out-the-money

In-the-money is a *win*. It means that you have made the right investment decision and earned a profit. On the contrary, out-the-money means that you have lost your wager.

Long-term option

In options trading, you get to choose how long a trade will last (expiration date). A long-term option simply refers to a trade that is long as 24 hours or more. A long-term option can last for a day, weeks, and months.

Speed option

As the name already implies, speed options are trades that last for a short period of time. This can be as fast as 30 seconds, a minute, or up to five to fifteen minutes, depending on the platform that you use.

Assets

Assets are valuable financial instruments. In options trading, you do not have to purchase any asset, you just have to determine if the value of an asset will be greater than or lower than its current price at the expiration time.

When trading binary options, the following assets are traded:

- stocks

- index

- commodities

- currency pairs

Bear market vs. bull market

On the one hand, a bear market means that the prices of certain assets are decreasing or are about to decrease. On the other hand, a bull market means that the prices of certain assets are increasing or are about to increase.

Take note, however, that even though a bear market is considered a negative sentiment, it does not affect you as a trader. In fact, you can even profit from it. This is because options trading has a dual nature: You can make a good amount of profit whether the price of certain underlying assets increase or decrease, provided you choose the right option (Call vs. Put).

Brokers and trading platforms

Before you can start trading binary options, you need to open an account with a broker. You can find many brokers when you make a search online. However, you need to choose a broker that will best suite your needs. Unfortunately, there are also scammers out there, so it is best to work only with a broker that has a well-established reputation.

Here is a list of trusted brokers. Take note that trading platforms may change their policies and management team. Therefore, even the most trusted brokers may no longer be a good choice tomorrow. Before you open an account, check the latest ratings and reviews given by other traders.

- iq option (www.iqoption.com)

- OptionRobot (www.optionrobot.com)

- Automated Binary (www.automatedbinary.com)

- Finpari (www.finpari.com)

- 24option (www.24option.com)

- fortuneJack (www.fortunejack.com) *bitcoin casino with binary options*

Important note:

Be sure to check the *banking options*. Many brokers accept many methods to make a deposit but only have limited options for making a withdrawal.

CHAPTER 2: RISKS & BENEFITS

Like any business venture, there are a number of risks and benefits associated with options trading. Here are the things that you can expect:

Market risk

The market is composed of real people. This is why it is extremely volatile. And, although there are methods that have been developed to predict market movements, there is no guaranteed way to determine how the market responds.

Lack of ownership

In options trading, you only wager on the future valuation of an underlying asset. Therefore, you do not exercise any right of ownership over any stock or asset.

High-risk investment

Like any other business that offers a high reward, the risk involved is also high. Unlike in trading stocks where you get to keep a losing stock with an opportunity that its price will soon increase or at least sell the stock to cut down your losses, you do not get to keep anything if you encounter a loss in options trading. In options trading, when you lose a trade, you lose the whole amount that you wager on that particular trade.

Limited opportunity

In options trading, the potential payout is already fixed even before you commence a trade. You cannot get a profit higher than the fixed payout. In forex or stock trading, the potential profit is almost limitless.

No liquidity

There is no liquidity because you do not have ownership of the stock or asset being traded. When you commence a trade, you just have to wait for the trading period to end and hope for the best. However, liquidity should not be an issue. After all, there are trades that can last for just a day, even less.

Losing is normal

Although there are people who rake in serious profits with options trading, the majority of traders lose their money, and they lose it within a short period of time.

If your entrepreneurial spirit remains strong and convinced despite the risks that you will encounter along your journey, then it is time for you to know the notable benefits of options trading.

The Benefits

High Return

For those who engage in forex or stock trading, a 50% is already considered high. And, usually, they would have to wait for months just to get a 50% profit. Most of the time, they do not even reach 50%. With options trading, getting a 90% per trade is normal. You can double your money in less than an hour.

Simplicity

It is the beautiful simplicity of options trading that makes it very attractive. You do not need to have any trading portfolio or any gambling experience. You can learn and start earning money with options trading almost instantly.

Fixed payout

Unlike other investment opportunities where you do not know how much money you can make, options trading lets you know the exact amount that you can profit before you commence a trade.

Quick turnover rate

Options trading allows you to choose just how long you want a trade to last. With speed trading, you can make multiple trades in less than five minutes.

Asset variety

Since you do not have to purchase any asset or currency, you have all the available underlying assets to choose from. Also, the minimum amount per trade is usually low, so you can easily diversify the assets that you invest in.

Controlled risk

You do not have to worry about hidden charges or surcharges. Whatever amount that you spend for a particular trade is your total risk. If you just want to risk $100, then simply invest $100, and there is nothing else that you should worry about.

Instant trading

Most established brokers offer a mobile phone feature. This will allow you to manage your account and commence a trade anytime and anywhere.

CHAPTER 3: STRATEGIES

Most people who lose their money with options trading either have no strategy at all and just rely on pure luck, or have a poor and underdeveloped strategy. If you want to rake in serious profits with options trading, you need to have a solid strategy. Unlike casino games where you simply have to vary the amount of your bets, success in options trading requires serious research, analysis, and practice.

Fundamental analysis

Fundamental analysis is considered the lifeblood of investment. This is the key to increasing your chances of making a profit. Remember that the market is run by real people and businesses, In fundamental analysis, you need to gather various information and analyze the economy, financial statements of businesses, as well as the latest news, among others. By analyzing these data, you can come up with a better investment decision. For example, if there is a report that the problem of the high unemployment rate has just been resolved in the U.S., and all other things being normal, then you can expect the value of the U.S. currency to increase.

If you like numbers, then fundamental analysis is the way to go. However, it is not recommended for speed options. This is because economic and business changes take time. It is best to use this method for trades that last for more than 12 hours.

Technical analysis

If you do not like analyzing lots of numbers, then technical analysis may be for you. Technical analysis is more visual. You will be analyzing charts and graphs. Technical analysis is excellent for fast trading or speed options. The proper way to use this method is to view the available graphs and look for patterns.

A note about patterns: Patterns depend on the latest trend. Is it a bull or a bear market? The risk here is that trends are not permanent. They change —and they usually change quickly. The key here is to find a pattern and be able to place your wager just before the trend changes.

Algorithmic and signals

By using computer programs and apps that can be installed on your computer, you will know where to invest in. This is an easy and quick way to come up with a decision; however, this method is not recommended because it is unreliable. There is simply no computer program that can accurately read the market's movement. However, this can be useful as secondary information.

Co-integration trading

This strategy uses the correlation that is created between two underlying assets. This usually occurs when two assets are in the same industry or have the same market. Due to their high correlation, you will notice that their prices are always close to each other. Hence, when a sudden significant gap appears between their prices, there is the highest probability that their prices will soon be close to each other again. So, you either place a Call option on the stock whose value has dropped or a Put option on the stock with a higher price.

Aggressive betting

As the name already implies, it is aggressive when you wager a big percentage of your total investment per trade, like wagering 20% per trade. Of course, the most aggressive way is to wager your whole investment on a single trade, but such is not recommended.

A famous aggressive betting strategy that is widely used by gamblers is known as the Martingale. This is where you double your wager after every loss. For example, first, you wager $10. If you lose the trade, you then wager $20. If you lose the trade again, you next wager $40, and so on… until you win a trade. When you win a trade, you go back to your initial wager of $10.

Although the Martingale looks feasible and reasonable, it is not effective in the long run. Unfortunately, it is not surprising to experience a series of wrong investment decisions. If you get really unlucky, you may even make 10 wrong decisions in a row. There only use this strategy for a short term, and be sure to back it up with sufficient research.

Conservative betting

Your betting strategy is considered conservative if you only use a small percentage of your total investment per trade, preferably just around 1%-3%. This is good if you already have a well-developed strategy that has a high rate of success.

Corrective

This is a good strategy to use when you see a sudden and significant increase or decrease in price, especially when such price spike is not clearly justified by existing factors. In such a case, you can expect for the price to balance out by reverting to its original value prior to the price spike, or somewhat close to it.

Breakout

This strategy works well with currency pairs. When a currency pair follows a tight or close price difference, and if you see them break out, the probability is high that their prices will continue to breakout. Although they will most likely revert to their normal price range, such will take time.

Asset mastery

Pick any underlying asset of your choice. Now, find out everything that you can about your chosen asset. Follow on the news and gather as much data as you can about that asset. Do this on a regular basis, preferably daily. You will notice that the more you know about a particular asset, the better predictions you can make. This also confirms that the market does not move at random.

CHAPTER 4: KEYS TO SUCCESS

Regardless whether you only want to trade for profit or for fun, you should know the best practices that can help increase your chances of success and minimize your losses.

Money management

No matter how well developed your strategy is or how much you have increased your success rate, you can lose your investment if you fail to manage your money properly. Also, do not use the money that you need to cover your household bills and other obligations. Do not forget that options trading is a high-risk investment.

Cash out

An important part of money management is learning to cash out. Unfortunately, many traders do not cash out their profits. Although it is good to grow your funds, you should still cash out from time to time. Take note that your profits only become real when you turn them into real cash; otherwise, they are nothing but numbers on a screen and almost have no difference with demo credits. Therefore, always cash out, you do not have to cash out everything, if you want, you can just cash out 20% of your profits on a regular basis.

Research and analysis

The possibility of doing a research and analysis is what separates options trading from gambling. You need to research and be updated on the news about the businesses themselves, as well as the factors that affect business performance. When analyzing, you need to drop your personal preferences and see everything as they are. Your investment decision must be based on facts without any bias. Research is key. Remember that the outcome of every trade and the movements of the graphs are mere reflections of reality. The more you know about the economy, real people, and real businesses, the better you can make an investment decision.

Focus on the assets

Although the graphs and charts may reveal to you certain patterns, it is worth noting that such patterns are not always present. And, many times, they do not stay for so long. After all, trends are meant to change, considering that the market is alive and continues to move. When making an investment decision, be sure that you have good information on the asset that is the subject of your trade. It must be emphasized that the more you know about a particular asset, the higher is the probability of making the right investment decision.

The importance of keeping a journal

Although having a journal is not a requirement, writing a trading journal can be very helpful. You do not need to be a professional writer; you only need to be open and honest when you write your journal.

A journal will allow you to think outside the box and be a better trader. You can write anything in your journal. You can write about your new learnings, mistakes, or any adjustments that you make to your strategy. Should you decide to use a journal, be sure to update it regularly

Start small

It can be very tempting to invest a lot in a particular trade when you know that you have researched a great deal just to make that trade. However, if you are a beginner, it is best to start small and focus on increasing your success rate. First, you need to get a feel of options trading and develop your strategy. If it is your first time to trade, do not focus on making money right away. After all, once you have enough experience and confidence, you can easily increase the amount that you invest per trade. To have a good and steady profit, aim to have a success rate of at least 60%-70%.

Focus on the numbers

There are ways to somehow manipulate the stocks for a short period of time. Especially these days when you can easily and quickly send a message to the world with just a few clicks of a mouse, some people are able to make their stocks look more attractive than they really are. Unfortunately, even the media may have its own preferences and prejudices. And many so-called "experts" on options trading cannot be trusted. Therefore, you need to focus on the numbers. Words are easy to manipulate and misinterpret, but numbers do not lie. When numbers are unduly manipulated, such fraudulent scheme tends to be obvious.

Do not chase after your losses

When you engage in options trading, you should be prepared to encounter some losses. You cannot expect to make the right investment decisions all the time. Losses are part of this kind of investment. The important thing is that the outcome of all your trades results in a positive profit.

Never chase after your losses. If you do, there is a higher risk of losing more money. Instead, be positive and focus on your profits, and how to profit some more.

Most people chase after their losses by increasing the amount of their wager per trade. This is risky because your strategy may not be suited for an aggressive betting, and your funds may not be enough to handle such big wagers.

Develop your strategy

In options trading, developing a strategy simply does not end. This is because you are dealing with a living and continuously evolving market. Therefore, you should continuously work on your strategy. It must be flexible enough to adapt to market changes and effective enough to make a decent amount of profit.

Have your own understanding of the market

True experts do not have the same strategy or share the same viewpoints all the time. They are experts because they have developed their own understanding of the market, and they can justify their views no matter how odd they may be. In the same manner, you also need to develop your own understanding of options trading and the market. In the beginning, you can rely on expert tips and advice, but soon you need to have your own way of making an investment decision. After all, nobody can get rich just by relying on expert advice. Also, out of the many people out there who claim to be "experts," only a few of them are true experts. Most of these "experts" have more losses than profits.

Practice

The only way to truly learn options trading is by actual practice. It is experience that will make you a real binary options trader. Take note that practicing does not only mean making a series of trades. In options trading, placing a trade is the easiest part. True practice means doing research and studying the various underlying assets, businesses, as well as the market behavior, among others.

PART IV

Chapter 1: Understanding the Fundamentals of

Position Trading

There are investors who get into investing for the long haul. These are long-term investors, and their approach is known as "position trading." Position trading is a long-term approach that looks to engage in holding on to assets for an extended period of time. If you are patient and in no hurry to make quick profits, you may consider position trading as an option for you.

Position is a logical progression from swing trading. The reason for this is that it takes quite a bit of foresight to determine what a stock will do in six months' time. That takes a lot of research and understanding of the market. If you are unfamiliar with the dynamics of a given market or the companies that comprise it, you may have a hard time "timing" the movements of these stocks or assets.

Difference Between Position Trading and Swing/Day Trading

Position trading differs from day and swing trading insofar as the timeframe that positions remain open. To give you a parameter of comparison, day trading refers to opening and closing positions within the same trading day. Swing trading generally implies keeping positions open for roughly a week at a time. As for position trading, the usual yardstick is anything beyond 10 days to approximately 200 days. The reason for this parameter is the moving averages that are calculated. Based on this consideration, position investors look at the 20, 50, and 100-day moving average.

Based on the parameters offered by these moving averages, position investors can then determine how long they plan to keep their positions open based on the anticipated shifts in price action. However, if the investor sees that their anticipated movements happen sooner, they may be perfectly willing to liquidate their position earlier than expected.

For instance, a position investor anticipates that a stock will double in price in a period of about three months. However, the company performed better than expected, which led to them doubling their share price in two months. A savvy position investor would cash out at this time. Sure, greed might kick in at this point, thus tempting the investor to stay in longer. However, there is no telling what could happen beyond the anticipated price point. So, it's best to cash out and then consider taking up another position, this time at a higher price point.

This type of assessment is made not just on the technical data that you find in charts. It's also made as a result of a combination of fundamental analysis and other specific data on the company. Position investors like to get as much information as they can on companies. They'll even go as far as trying to talk to people on the inside to see what's going on.

This is why position investing is a very serious deal.

Reasons for Investing Long-Term

Long-term investing boils down to two factors. The first is maximizing profit as much as possible. The second is preserving wealth.

Let's look at the first reason.

Position investors are keen on making large profits on individual deals. They are not keen on making short-term profits. In the short-term, you stand to make pennies on the dollar. That's not bad, especially if you engage in high-frequency trading. But when it comes to hitting home runs, you have to stay in the game long enough. For instance, you cannot expect a company's stock price to double in a matter of hours. But, you can expect it to double in a matter of weeks. As a result, you stand to clean up is something like this happens.

The second reason is preserving wealth. Often, investors find themselves with extra cash. Having extra cash can be a problem, especially if it's not producing anything. Now, it's one thing to have an emergency savings fund that's sitting there waiting to be your rescue boat in case of emergency. However, there comes a point where having money sitting idly in a bank account becomes unproductive. So, investors are keen to place these funds into longer-term investments that would enable them to keep their money working for them.

It should be noted that long-term investing is not for everyone. In particular, it can be a great option for you if you have money that you are not looking to use any time soon. This is why the safest long-term investment is bonds. When you buy bonds, for example, 6-month or one-year bonds, you are putting your money in a safe spot. While the returns may not blow your mind, you know your money is both safe and generating a return.

That's a lot better than keeping under your mattress.

Advantages of Long-Term Investing

The upside to long-term investing boils down to the following three reasons:

1. Potential for profit is substantial

As stated earlier, position investors set themselves up for considerable gains. When playing their cards right, they can cash in trend reversals, market swings, and the changes in investors' psyche. This is why the profit which can be made on a single deal can be far more substantial than the profits made through high-frequency trading. In fact, traders look at day trading as a means of keeping the lights on while looking to position investing as a means of getting rich.

2. It's less risky

When you invest in the right instruments, such as government bonds, the potential for risk is a lot lower. In the case of bonds, the only way you could lose your money is if the government went belly up. Unless you buy bonds from not-so-reputable countries, your money will be safe. This is why long-term investing can be a lot less risky when compared to being fully invested in stocks.

3. It's less time consuming

Long-term investing requires a great deal of upfront research. But once you have completed the research needed to take your positions, then you can lay back and simply keep track of the situation. This means that you can devote your attention to other investments or other types of trading, such as day and/or swing trading. In fact, seasoned vets engage in all three types of trading. Naturally, that all depends on the overall amount of time you can devote to trading in addition to the investment capital you have on hand.

Drawbacks of Long-Term Investing

When it comes to long-term investing, there are also drawbacks that need to be considered.

1. Much more capital is needed

This is the biggest issue with position trading. Day traders can make a go start with very little money as they are consistently using the same capital over and over. This is why high-frequency traders can double their money in a short period of time. In long-term investing, much more capital is needed because money is parked for a much longer time period. This is especially true if you are looking to make a huge deal. Position investors generally invest thousands of dollars per trade as opposed to a couple of hundred that day traders may allocate. While there is no requisite number, a good ballpark for position trading is to be at least in the six-figure range. Naturally, you will not invest all of it in a single deal; you will need this kind of money to ensure you make it big.

2. Time is a huge factor

Time is the biggest issue when it comes to long-term investing. If you are in need of making quick profits, then this approach is not for you. Ideally, you would allocate money into long-term investments that you don't actually need. Now, that might sound funny at the moment. But the fact of the matter is that high-level investors reach a point in which they have money they don't need. So, these funds are ideal for long-term investing.

3. A good deal of experience is needed

The reason why long-term investing is not recommended to novice investors is due to the fact that investors need to be cognizant of what the market may or may not do. This type of instinct can only be sharpened with time and experience. As a result, novice investors may find it very difficult to truly gauge what the markets will do over an extended period of time.

Stocks to Hold for Long-Term

This is a question for the ages. Stocks to hold on to for the long haul are the so-called "blue chip" stocks. These are proven winners which have a solid track record. They are also usually very expensive. Nevertheless, when you are able to buy into them, you will find that the return on them is far greater than the bulk of the market.

If you find it unaffordable at this point to get into blue-chip stocks, you might consider an index fund. These funds can be invested specifically in blue-chip companies. Consequently, you don't need to actually own any stock. Rather, you are getting exposure to these stocks. While the returns might be lower than if you actually traded the stocks themselves, you would still be getting solid returns, particularly if you are planning on investing money that you don't need right away.

Now, if you are able to afford individual shares of these companies, you can buy up as many as you can and hold on to them, especially during market downturns. Since investors generally panic, they will try to buy up as many of the best stocks. This is where you cash in. In fact, if you can anticipate a market downturn well ahead of time, you can buy up blue-chip stocks at current market prices and then flip them to hungry investors when the downturn occurs.

Chapter 2: Fundamentals of Position Trading

When it comes to position trading, there are a series of elements that comprise its fundamentals. As a position investor, you need to be aware of these. Otherwise, you run the risk of missing out on the underlying principles that will ensure that you make the most of your investment capital.

In this chapter, we are going to take a look at these fundamentals and what you need to do in order to capitalize on them. By the end of this chapter, you'll be able to determine if position trading is right for you. At the very least, you will determine if it is something you want to work your way up to. After all, you can juggle all three types of investment approaches discussed in this book.

Additionally, It's critical that you are totally familiar with the basic components of position trading. That way, you can begin to frame your mindset in both short-term and long-term visions. That way, you can make the most of your skills and experience. At the end of the day, the only limitation you will find is your investment capital.

Use of Technical Analysis and Fundamental Analysis in Position Trading

It goes without saying that technical analysis is absolutely critical in position trading. Without it, you really have no way of knowing what an individual stock may or may not. Moreover, you have no way of knowing what the market, as a whole, stands to do. This is why technical analysis must become your guiding beacon.

Beyond the cold numbers in terms of stock quotes, technical analysis allows you to gain insight into historical data on individual stocks. This is important to note as historical data can help you backtest your assumptions. Likewise, backtesting can also help you disprove claims made by analysts or experts.

As for fundamental analysis, the influence that political, social, and cultural factors can exert over the markets in a longer period of time can be quite considerable. This is why position traders do their best to keep tabs the events around them.

As a general rule of thumb, please keep an eye on economic indicators. Figures on employment, payrolls, consumer confidence, GDP, and sales reports, in addition to corporate earnings, are all indicators that will help you gain a sense of what investors are looking to do, both in the short and long term.

Lastly, if you have the chance to talk to other investors, do so. In this regard, we're talking about regular investors who work for themselves or have perhaps hired professional money managers. It's always great to talk shop and exchange notes. Who knows that information you might be able to dig up? Plus, getting a sense of what other investors are thinking is a great way to gauge your strategy. This will allow you to assess your own strategy in such a way that you can fine-tune any aspects which you may have overlooked.

Long-Term Investment Instruments

Once you have determined that long-term investing works for you, it's important to figure out where to allocate your money. In this regard, it's worth looking into the various types of instruments in which you can place your money. We will begin by talking about the safest and moving on to the riskiest.

The safest long-term investment is government bonds. There is no question about it. Government bonds, particularly issued by stable countries, can provide you with the assurance you need. And while the returns aren't always mind-blowing, bonds pay more than the average investment account.

As for corporate bonds, these are highly risky. Even with blue-chip companies, there is no assurance that they will endure into the long-term. There have been many cases in which industry leaders go belly-up. So, corporate bonds always have a higher risk than government bonds. However, corporate bonds do pay a higher yield. Hence, it's a question of assessing just how risk the corporation truly is.

Then, index and mutual funds are a great way of parking your money in a long-term passive investment. They produce a higher yield than bonds. Additionally, they offer the opportunity for diversification. Mutual and index funds are also good if you want to day trade while setting some additional money aside for other purposes. You could save up money for a down payment on a house by stashing in an index fund. You would just have to negotiate the term so that you can access it reasonably quickly.

You can also make long-term investments by holding actual stock. It should be noted that index funds don't represent ownership of any kind of stock. So, when you buy real shares of a company, you are exposing yourself to the performance of that particular firm. This is why we encourage investors to look for blue-chip companies as much as possible. However, if you are keen on taking on money risk, you can look at lower-tier companies which have a good upside. These companies may provide solid returns, especially if they are poised to make a significant jump in their respective market.

Lastly, there are ETFs. ETFs are risky because their performance is tied to an asset such as a commodity. As a result, there is no real way you can guarantee their performance. In fact, you may be overwhelmed by the returns an ETF can generate while other times, it may fall flat. This is why you need to be cognizant of the underlying asset in the ETF and how you can profit from it. Most investors who choose to allocate their funds into ETFs choose highly liquid assets such as oil or currencies.

Please note that there is the derivatives market. These types of instruments, such as mortgage-backed securities, are highly risky and generally highly leveraged. Please refrain from investing in these instruments unless you are totally aware of their implications. Since they can be quite complex, we recommend that you do your due diligence on these before investing.

Identifying Long-Term Trend

Long-term trend can be tricky to spot. The reason for this is that you need to look at the right timeframe in order to properly assess a trend. This is why position investors like to look at the various types of moving average. You can start with the 10-day moving average and try to spot a trend. Generally, you should be able to see one even at this point. However, don't be surprised if you only manage to see a sideways trend. At the 10-day mark, this is quite normal.

Then, the next step is to look at the 20-day moving average. At this point, you should be able to clearly see a trend. It might still look sideways, but this timeframe should allow you to get a good sense of where the long-term direction is heading.

The next two timeframes are crucial is spotting a long-term trend. The 50-day moving average is a great indicator of where prices sit. However, then compared to the 200-day moving average, you can really see if there is confirmation of trend, or if there is a trend reversal.

To do this, you need to use the MACD as a means of confirming continuation or reversal. The easiest way to spot a trend reversal is when the 50-day moving average cross over the 200-day moving average. Now, you might see the 10-day and 20-day moving averages intersect, but there are only short-term movements. They may have very little bearing on the long-term trend. That's why position investors pay very close attention to the 50 and 200-day moving averages. As long as these two moving averages do not cross over, then you have a continuation of trend.

Once the 50-day and 200-day moving average have crossed over, then you may find divergence in these prices. In some cases, both moving averages may run parallel to one another. In other cases, you may have a very clear divergence. When these two lines run relatively parallel to one another, it means that investors aren't totally sure of which direction they will head. However, if you see a clear divergence, then you know where investors are heading.

To further cement your analysis, check out the candlesticks. These will confirm the direction in which prices are heading. If you happen to spot short candlesticks, you are seeing unsure investors. However, long candlesticks are a good indication that investors know where they want to go.

Ignoring Short-Term Gains

Since position trading is all about keeping tabs on what's going on regularly, you might find that there are significant fluctuations on a day to day basis. In fact, you might be really encouraged to see spikes in price, such as in a head and shoulders pattern. But, please be advised that these spikes may only be indicative of short-term movements.

You see, investors who are playing the short-term game generally get caught up in the hype that surrounds stocks. After all, they are looking to ride the waves and make short-term windfall profits. As a position investor, you are not looking at the short-term gains. In fact, you could both day and position trade a stock, but that shouldn't cloud your judgment as to the overall price action.

Unless you see a massive gain in a long-term position, it's best to resist the temptation of cashing out early. The problem with doing this is that once a stock reaches a certain price point, you won't be able to get into at a lower price point unless you waited for it to come back down. However, there is no telling when that may happen. So, if you get into a stock at a very low price point, it's best to hold on to it as long as it takes to reach your desired price point.

For instance, you pick up a stock at $5 a share. You anticipate it will hit $20 in roughly eight weeks' time. By week five, it spikes from $7 to $15. At this point, you are tempted to sell and re-enter the position. Sure, you'll make a tidy profit, but then you won't be able to get into the position at the same $5 price point. You might end up getting in at $14 or $15. At this point, you might feel that you'll still make a profit when it hits $20.

But what if it doesn't?

This is where you would be taking unnecessary risk. Unless the stock suddenly jumped to $25 after five weeks, it's best to hold on to it until it reaches your desired price point.

Spotting Long-Term Breakouts

Long-term breakouts depend on both technical analysis and instinct. There are times when companies get stuck at a certain share price because they are unable to improve their sales or generate the hype needed to get investors to take a chance on them. Then, there are companies that are perennial underachievers. But, there are companies that poised to breakout. These are the companies that have great products in the pipeline or are highly disruptive in their respective field. These can also be up and coming stars that have a product or technology that hasn't been perfect yet.

These companies are the ones that you want to get into in the early going. They may have shares trading at ridiculously low prices. So, they may be worth taking a flyer on. If they really do take off, then you will make a killing on their stock once it soars. There is the possibility that such companies never deliver on their promise. In which case, you may have to make an assessment on whether they are worth holding on to or not.

As for blue-chip companies, the technical data will reveal everything you really need to know. Since we're are talking about well-established companies, there really isn't much guesswork. Still, it could be that they provide you with innovations that could lead to a long-term breakout. This is why conducting thorough research may lead you to uncover an unexpected boost. So do keep this in mind when looking into established market leaders.

Chapter 3: Building Wealth Through Position

Trading

Throughout this book, we've mentioned how day trading is intended to keep the lights on. In other words, day trading is meant to be a trading approach that can produce enough profits to help you make the most of your finances by supplementing your income. In fact, day trading is not meant to replace your day job, especially if you earn a decent wage.

However, when you put day and swing trading, you may be able to replace your regular wage and dedicate your time and attention to trading as a full-time career. Plenty of folks have done it. So, it's definitely a question of making sense of the various options at your disposal.

With that in mind, you can use position trading to actually build wealth. By "building wealth," we mean making the most of your abilities and skills to accumulate money, among other assets. You see, when you hold stock of valuable companies, you know that you are going to be in a good position no matter what the market is like. While other investors are getting wiped out by a market downturn, you are in a position to stay afloat.

So, let's take a look at three ways in which position trading can help you build wealth.

Protection Against Shifts in the Market

When you are invested mainly in blue-chip stocks or safer assets such as bonds, short-term shifts should not affect you. Unless there was a seismic shift in the market, you would find that holding these assets will protect the bulk of your wealth in the long-term. Plus, blue-chips and bonds are highly liquid. This means that if you ever needed money in a pinch, you could easily sell them to raise cash. That's why you will find that most investors like to have an allocation to these assets. Recommended allocations range from 10% to 20% bonds (depending on prevailing market conditions) and somewhere around a 25% allocation for blue-chips.

In addition, some investors like to have exposure to commodities such as oil or gold. You can do this by means of ETFs. Generally speaking, 5% to 10% allocation to commodities works rather well. So, do take the time to consider what this asset class can do for you.

Diversification Against Risk

Diversification is the ultimate hedge against risk. This is why you need to make sure that you have your portfolio spread out across the various asset classes we have discussed. Investors who dabble in all three levels of trading like to maintain the bulk of their assets in long-term investments. These investors like to leave about a quarter of their investment capital allocated specifically to day and swing trading. Please note that you don't need to allocate significant funds toward day trading since you don't need a great deal of investment capital to make in short-term, high-frequency trading.

Additionally, adjusting your allocation according to current market conditions is a must. You cannot expect to build wealth by setting your investments on autopilot. This is a passive investment approach that would require you to hire a professional money manager. If you are keen on setting your investments on autopilot, then you might want to consider buying into index funds and ETFs that don't require you to play an active role. That way, you can use your time to research other types of instruments, which could yield positive results for you.

Maintaining a Balanced Portfolio

A balanced portfolio depends on what you are looking to achieve. Some investors start out with a much larger capital. So, their main goal is to preserve their wealth over the long haul. Other investors start out with very little capital. As such, they are looking to build their way up.

Based on your starting point, you can afford to be more or less aggressive. On the whole, smaller investors tend to be much more aggressive as they have a lot more ground to make up. This is why day trading is always the best place to start for smaller investors.

Nevertheless, maintaining a balanced portfolio essentially depends on current market conditions. For instance, when the stock market is booming, it makes sense to have a larger allocation to stocks. By the same token, when the stock market is going through a bear market, it's best to reduce your overall exposure to non-blue-chip stocks.

When the stock market is booming, investors like to be aggressive. This implies taking a chance on startups and new IPOs. When things are going well, high-level investors tend to pull out of index funds and ETFs and go straight into direct stock ownership. You stand to make more money by flipping stock itself since there is any number of investors looking to get in.

In contrast, high-level investors seek shelter in other types of investments, like gold and bonds, when the market is going through a downturn. Whenever you are investing in a bear market, you need to put your money into highly liquid asset classes (FOREX counts in this category, too) so that you can liquidate them in a short timeframe. Please bear in mind that cash is king in a bear market. This is why investors like to have long-term but liquid assets. Instruments like 401(k)s and mutual funds won't help you weather the storm. With these instruments, the only real choice you have is to wait for the storm to pass.

When looking at long-term investing, consider how important it is to preserve wealth. It's one thing to build wealth, but it's another entirely different thing to preserve it. This is why you need to focus on what it takes to keep the money you have worked hard to make. At the end of the day, your ability to preserve your wealth is something that you can pass down from generation to generation. This is why you need to think about what it means to be a successful investor today and into the future.

PART V

Chapter One: Investments with Block Chain

The business models of several different companies in a wide range of sectors have been transformed by block chain. Looking at block chain, you are going to see that it appears to be a digital spreadsheet that is being worked on by members inside of an organization. The "digital spreadsheet" is going to be on a decentralized network.

Due to the way that block chain is written, it has some unique factors that are not going to be able to be understood, even by the investors that think that they can make a profit on that technology. Block chain is not like traditional trading because it has several different levels that are used.

Block chain offers at least five different ways that you can make an investment that will benefit you later on.

1. Stockpile coins

Many investors are stockpiling gold so that they can wait to sell it whenever the price goes up sometime in the future. However, there are other investors that are stockpiling bitcoins. Stockpiling gold and stockpiling bitcoins are going to each have their advantages as well as their disadvantages but what it comes down to is the supply and demand. Whenever the supply is limited, the demand is going to go up, therefore, the value is going to increase which is going to be the opportune time to sell what it is that they are stockpiling.

2. Penny stocks

Penny stocks are a cryptocurrency like bitcoins just like Ether is a cryptocurrency, but they all work on a different system due to the fact that they are competing with bitcoin.

3. Crowdfunding with altcoin

Crowdfunding is a method that you can use whenever you are trying to raise capital for an investment. The coins are not going to need to be used when you are dealing with crowdfunding. Instead, people are going to give you coins before you start mining which is typically done before a system is opened to the public.

4. Angel funding and start up ventures

Block chain makes it possible for a great number of entrepreneurs and investors to come together and find each other to get funding.

5. Pure block chain technology

The technology behind block chain is on the rise, and the companies that are taking advantage of it are getting their name out there so that they can be better known whenever you find the block chain technology everywhere. A company by the name of Global Arena Holdings uses the block chain technology as leverage in getting their votes verified.

Chapter Two: Implementing Block Chain

Knowing how you want to use block chain is vital before you get too deep into it. Block chain offers two ways to use their system, but ensure that you are choosing the one that is best for you. Typically people use block chain with an individual account.

With an individual account, you need to set up your wallet. Your wallet is going to be where you keep all of your bitcoins and will run off of most mobile devices and computers. Digital wallets are more secure than real wallets because they are not going to be stolen and they are most likely not going to be hacked.

When you use a software wallet, you are not going to be required to have a third party service for the wallet to be downloaded. Once it has been placed on your computer, you are going to have all of your transactions at your fingertips.

Next, you need to acquire bitcoins. You have the option to trade bitcoins for goods or services that you may be able to offer to those in the bitcoin system; however, it is hard to find someone who is willing to trade bitcoins because they do not want to give up their coins. You can also buy bitcoins in the marketplace where you can spend real world money and purchase as many coins as you want.

Lastly, you have the option to mine coins. Programs can be placed on your computer that will use a CPU that is customized to assist you in making a quick profit without you having to do many of anything.

You should make sure that your wallet is secured! Encrypt your wallet so that you are not leaving it open to hackers who want to steal your coins. If your coins are stolen, or bitcoin does not offer you an option where they will replace them because they are your responsibility.

Bitcoins can be spent just like regular money can be. However, you need to find a merchant who will accept bitcoins as payment.

Chapter Three: Smart Contracts

Smart contracts are probably going to be the aspect of block chain that will most likely be championed in the future. A smart contract is just a type of computer code that is activated once the block chain as a whole register that a predetermined incident has occurred. The smart contract is then given its own block and distributed as part of the chain.

While it may seem complicated, you can think of them in much the same way certain functions in a checking account work. In most checking accounts, automated deductions can be set up either by the user or by a third party with the user's permission. A smart contract works in broadly the same way but from a decentralized—not centralized--position. Put another way; a smart contract is the computer code equivalent of the legalese in a contract that stipulates how and when all the little details are carried out.

Additionally, as long as the smart contract is generated on a public block chain, then, unlike in the banking example, there is no third party (such as the bank) who is able to step in and actively prevent the transaction from occurring. The transaction is equally secure if it is performed by a bank or by a block chain. This is due to the extreme type of security that is built into the block chain model, the fact that the data is decentralized, and the extreme cost required to hijack a block chain.

What's more, unlike with traditional contracts, smart contracts that are executed via block chain are completely public and viewable by anyone with a copy of the chain. This means that the smart contract is never open for debate or discussion; it is purely an expression of the facts as they are truly stated. This can be seen as a miracle or a curse, of course, depending on the nature of the information being made public.

A smart contract is where a computer protocol can facilitate, verify, and even enforce the negotiation and performance of a contract in which the contractual clause becomes unnecessary.

The smart contract can also have a user interface that will emulate the logic of a contractual clause(s). The proponents of a smart contract claim that many different kinds of the contractual clauses may thus be made partial or even fully self-executing, self-enforcing, or possibly even both.

Smart contracts are going to aim to provide the security that is superior to any traditional law contract. This will, therefore, reduce the transaction costs that are associated with the process of drawing up a contract.

Common usage cases

With the rising market penetration of various financial technologies, smart contracts are becoming more and more prevalent. A big reason for that is

116

because they are simplifying many common contract usage cases. For example, they are already making it easier for users to update various contract terms in real time, despite it taking days for physical copies to move back and forth to perform the same function. This not only improves the speed with which such processes can be performed but also greatly increases the odds of their accuracy remaining at acceptable levels throughout.

Smart contracts also activate automatically once certain real world conditions have been met, which means they require fewer resources to be utilized to the fullest. While this won't mean much to most users who use them infrequently, for business to business transactions, the savings will likely be substantial. The guaranteed and secure nature of a smart contract also means that it can be executed upon without the need for a third party to guarantee the transaction via escrow, reducing the closing costs of the contract on all sides.

Financial institutions will also find smart contracts useful in numerous ways. In regard to trade clearing or settlement scenarios, the final results relating to settlements, transfers, and trades is tallied automatically. Smart contracts can also be used when it comes to coupon payments, specifically to return principal on expired bonds. They also work with insurance claims as a means of minimizing errors and streamlining the flow of work between departments. Finally, they are also known to improve the regulation of Internet of Things services.

In the health care sector, smart contracts are known to offer up numerous advantages. For instance, they improve the accuracy with which medical records are updated as patients are transferred between departments. They can also be used to monitor the health of the population as a whole via public blockchains that update automatically and pay participants for using their information. Smart contracts are also already in use in many Internet of Things devices where they are used to determine the success of fitness goals and release rewards accordingly.

In the music industry, smart contracts are already being put to work tracking royalties for song usage and distributing payments accordingly. It is also being put to work on a smaller scale to enhance person to person interactions and is predicted to lead to things like trading energy credits and increased peer lending opportunities. This same technology is currently being adapted for use with the Tesla electric car, whereby users can charge at any charging station and be billed for the transaction automatically.

It is also changing the way large products are shipped and tracked by sending out automated documentation as various production pieces make their way through processing, and on to shipping. This can even be cued to the input of certain signatures, meaning the process is seamless for signing the contract to receiving the goods. Later on down the line, if there are questions about the quality of the shipment, then the entire route the product took from creation to delivery can be tracked. This is due to the fact that it is on the same block chain that enables the creation of the contract in the first place.

For credit enforcement, the smart contracts are becoming an extension of property law. The credit agreements are going to disable the product that you have purchased if you fail to make the payments that you agreed to make. For example, if you buy a new car on credit and fail to make your payment. Then the doors to your car are going to lock and then drive itself back to the showroom.

However, most electrical products come with what is known as a kill switch that can be disabled should a condition not be met between the two parties. This would happen if the payments were being made through a public channel such as cryptocurrency.

Chapter Four: Block Chain Pros and Cons

Block chain is not immune to have its pros and cons just like everything else that you can get involved in. While block chain is versatile, there are still those who are hesitant to switch over to the new technology when they can just stick to the methods they know work.

Block chain will protect your identity as well as work with you to make sure that your money is not stolen. Your personal information does not have to be entered into the block chain system in order for any transactions to be completed. It is going to be much like when you buy something with cash. You do not even have to enter a real email address. The block chain system gives you an email address, so that will change each time that you make a transaction on the system.

If there is any cost to send or receive a payment on the block chain system, it is not going to be a large fee. Any payments that go international will not force you to pay things such as transaction or exchange fees that a traditional financial institute would force you to do. Therefore, this will help keep all of your fees down when you find yourself traveling abroad.

One of the biggest cons that you are going to find with block chain is that you do not have the ability to reverse a transaction once you have made it. So, you need to be cautious when you are sending out coins because once it has been spent, there is a possibility that you are not going to get a refund from that person. Basically, keep a good handle on where you send your coins and have extra security on your system so that your coins cannot be stolen by a hacker.

Keeping your bitcoins means that you are going to have to deal with volatility. The value of bitcoins fluctuates with time and the longer you hold onto them, the less value they are going to hold when you are ready to spend them. So, you are going to be gambling with your coins and their value the longer that you hold onto them.

There are several companies such as Etsy and TigerDirect that are going to accept bitcoins as a form of payment rather than taking cash. However, big companies like Walmart and Target have not gotten on board yet, and there is no telling when they are going to get on board with bitcoin considering how well they are doing as it is. But, it is very likely that they are going to look into accepting bitcoins as the value of bitcoins goes up making it to where more and more people are using it.

Rather than being like a credit card, bitcoins are like cash. There are no extensions in the warranty that you have to deal with, but then again you are not going to have the rewards that you can get when it comes to using a credit card. Some places do not allow you to use a credit card for whatever policy reason that they have so then you are always going to worry about that as well. Then there are the fees and the added headache of if you do not pay it, it is going to affect your credit score.

Cash, on the other hand, is taken everywhere, there are no fees, in fact, there are many times that you end up getting a discount because you used cash. With bitcoin, you are going to be able to use it without the headache of late fees or other things that you are going to have to worry about with a credit card.

The biggest similarity that bitcoins has with credit cards is the fact that it is not going to be accepted everywhere.

On the business side of it, using bitcoin is going to save you money. If you are going to use services such as Coinbase, then the first million dollars that you make by accepting bitcoins is going to be free for you. It is from here that you are going to begin to pay at least one percent on all of the transactions that you do. However, this is still going to be considerably less than what you are paying in order to accept credit cards.

Exchanges that are doing with bitcoins can be converted easily without the need to worry about risking a lot of volatility. Not to mention, bitcoin eases any worries that you are going to have of chargebacks or even hackers getting into your system and stealing your customer's credit card numbers. The merchants that use bitcoin are normally going to work off of a tablet or even a smartphone when they are accepting a payment. This is an added benefit because you will not need a big fancy system that can only stay in one place. Therefore, you are going to be able to take your business with you anywhere and accept payments. Which is a major plus for your business!

CPSIA information can be obtained
at www.ICGtesting.com
Printed in the USA
LVHW012233261020
669863LV00027B/693

9 789814 952101